Young and Called

keep the faith

Young and Called

Jenice S. Borges

Young and Called
ISBN 9781453843406
Printed in the United States of America

Foreword: Pastor Veta L. Blanding
Preface: Minister Shari C. Madkins
Author Photo: Denise B. Obasi
Editorial services by Sandra K. Williams

Acknowledgements

I want to extend a big thank you to those who have poured into my life and shared in me being the person I am today.

Mother, Denise Borges; Grandmother, Barbara Borges; Brother, Jevon Standfield; Pastor Arnold Davis, Deborah Davis, Bishop William L. Sheals, First Lady Patricia Sheals and the Hopewell Missionary Baptist Church Family; Pastor Noble Williams, First Lady Dorothy Williams and the Greater Mt. Zion Baptist Church Family; Pastors Gerard and Veta Blanding; Pastor Keean Sutton; Prophetess Kim Williams; Faithful Followers Worldwide Ministries; to all my family and friends, you know who you are.

I would like to give a special thanks to all of you who sowed financially into this project and made this a dream come true for me. Because you have sown a seed, expect to receive a great harvest. May our Father in heaven continue to bless every endeavor of your life. I love you all very much:

Tony and Sophia Taylor
Taylor Funeral Home in Phenix City, Alabama
Pastor Arnold and Debbie Davis
Global Missions and Outreach Center in Norcross, Georgia
Pastor Noble Williams
Mary Cornish
Debra Searles
Wanda Sanchious
Barbara Borges
Jean Prioleau

5

Table of Contents

Foreword

If you are holding a copy of this book in your hand, consider yourself blessed. It is a great honor to write this foreword on behalf of someone that I consider as my own child. I have had the privilege of watching and seeing her testimony unfold before my very eyes. In this day and time of bad news, corrupt communication and negative press, this is an opportunity to read something that is not only quality, but life changing. Every situation that occurs in your life can work for your good if you allow it to. Jenice Borges is living proof that it can have a positive impact and push you into your destiny.

I met Jenice when she was a teenager and saw the hand of God upon her life. I have watched how her trials have made others strong. The first time I heard her speak to a vast audience was when she was only 16 and had just returned from a missionary trip to Haiti. Boy, was it powerful! A couple of years later, she became the youngest person to preach an initial sermon and the youngest to be ordained at Hopewell Missionary Baptist Church under the leadership of Bishop William Sheals.

Every child and adult enjoys being in the company of this young woman. I have seen a resilience and a joy in her that cannot be matched. How did she do it? I will let you decide after reading this book.

If you have a child, a teenager or a young adult (male or female), read this book, purchase a copy for your ministry leaders, as a gift for a graduate or an inspirational book for the youth. I have experienced the wisdom, knowledge and power that rests on this young lady and have seen the lives impacted by her ministry. *Young and Called* is not just a catchy title but it is her story and it can be your story as well.

I personally want to thank Jenice for having the courage and discipline to pen her story and bare her soul so that others can prosper. Giving to others and pouring yourself out unselfishly is consistent with you writing this book.

God bless you as you read these pages. I pray that it will impact, encourage, excite and motivate you to be the best that God has called you to be, no matter your age!

I love you Jenice!

Pastor Veta L. Blanding

Hopewell Missionary Baptist Church-North East

Preface

An interesting paradox is created when you make the request, "Lord use me!" - and the Lord actually answers, "Ok!" Many of us find ourselves in love with God and His purpose for the earth. We want to participate in the great plan of redemption, but we don't always know what that means. So when we feel God tugging at our hearts, it creates a range of emotions. We are filled with joy from knowing God has selected us for His special use, but tempered with despair because we feel inadequate to fulfill the call. Gratitude is often paired with resentment because we are humbled at the opportunity to serve, yet disappointed when this service interferes with our own plans for our life. Minister Jenice has traveled this road and knows the spiritual and emotional battles one faces when they are young and called. Her story is an encouraging call to action that will quell your fears and motivate you into action as you seek to fulfill God's will for your life.

Shari C. Madkins

Chapter One

The Beginning of the Journey

The Vision

I can remember it so plainly. It was one Saturday morning as I was lying in the bed. It was weird because typically I would sleep late on the weekends. I'd wake up fix a bowl of Froot Loops and get back in the bed and watch my favorite show "Ghostwriter". But this Saturday was different. I woke up to look at the clock and it was 7:00 in the morning. I was wondering to myself what in the world are you doing up. I tried to close my eyes and go back to sleep. This is when my life changed forever. As I closed my eyes I thought I was sleep, but I was awake. I realize now that I was in a trance. I saw myself standing before thousands of people. People were crying and lifting their hands in the air. There I was, standing on a podium with all black on, and I was preaching the Gospel with power. I immediately opened my eyes and laid there wondering what just happened. I began to pray to God and ask Him what it meant. For some strange reason I was compelled to write, so I grabbed my notebook and my pen and I began to write what I now know as a sermon. The first sermon I ever wrote "Stop in the Name of Love". I never preached it to anyone only to myself and the Lord over and over again that morning. I don't know where that two page sermon disappeared to. It dealt with people not giving God what He deserves, and treating the church like some sort of social club. I was compelling people to get right with God. I tucked it away and never told anyone about what happened to me that morning.

But I felt something strange within me, like I was different. I had an encounter with God that morning. The Father was showing me what my calling was. Again, I didn't know at that time it was a vision. I thought a vision was something like a cloud falling from heaven and angels coming to you and talking to you. I learned later that what I had been praying to God for had finally happened; I finally had a vision from God. I was 13 at the time this happened.

My family and I moved from Queens New York to Atlanta when I was nine years old. While we were in New York, my Grandmother took us to the Catholic Church she grew up in. I remember my little Rosary beads. I used to love lighting as many candles in the back of the church as I passed by heading to my seat. I was not supposed to do that, but I was a child, what do you expect. We used to sit on the hard pews with the kneeling benches below our feet. I never understood anything that was going on. The old hymns they sung sounded like it was a different language. I used to sleep most of the time, but I was in Church.

The time came around for my First Communion. My class had prepared for this day and we had to learn this speech as a class and everyone had a part. It was set up for two people to recite a line. Now let me paint a picture for you. I was a very quiet and shy kid and this was way out of my comfort zone. So there we all stood at the front of the church and we began our speech. When my time came I recited my part with no mistakes. I had boldness about me and there was no one else reciting it with me. My family was shocked and they could not stop talking about it. I was shocked! My grandmother and great grandmother said that there was something special about me and my ability to speak like that. As I reflect on that time of my life I see the stage was being set for what God had for me in the future.

When we moved to Atlanta we attended Hopewell Missionary Baptist Church. What a culture shock for me! I had never seen a church with drums, guitars, and people clapping. Most of all, the preacher was preaching with such power. The first time I saw people catch the Holy Spirit I was scared, I didn't know what to do. I didn't even know what the Holy Spirit was.

But it made me feel good on the inside. I would always get this tingling feeling flowing through my body when I went to church. I didn't know then, but I know now, it was the Holy Spirit. Since I was a real quiet kid I didn't say much, but I was always looking and observing my surroundings. I would never go to any of the kids' service. I always stayed in the main sanctuary. Shortly after we moved, we joined Hopewell and I gave my life to Christ. It was June of 1990. When my family went to the front to join, the pastor went down the line and asked if we were saved. I said yes. I didn't really know what it meant, but I knew it was the only way to get into heaven and I knew I didn't want to go to hell. They took us in the back where they explained salvation and gave me this kids' book on the process of salvation and what Jesus did for us. I read that book cover to cover when I got home. I was happy because I was not going to hell.

The Beginning of the Journey

We got into a routine that happens to a lot of people. We were going to church on Sunday; then on Wednesday for Bible Study. Like always, I was in the services with adults. Sometimes I was the only child, but I was getting it! I understood what was being taught to me at that level. I was gaining all this knowledge in the Word, but didn't know what to do with it.

As I was getting older and maturing in the word of God, I began thinking, there has to be more to this than just coming to church. What else can I do? I started asking the Lord, what else can I do, what am I supposed to do? The vision that I spoke of earlier was a response to that plea. In other words, I got what I asked for. At that time I didn't have the understanding, so I hid the secret God revealed to me in the inner chambers of my heart.

The Beginning of the Journey

Getting Involved

Because I was always with the adults, I didn't know any youth in the church. I was a loner and didn't like to talk to people. One day the youth minster approached me and asked me to come to youth service. I had always been able to dodge him and avoid eye contact. On another day, while I was minding my own business, I walked right in his path and could not avoid him any longer. I agreed to go to the youth service, but I just said it so he would leave me alone. It took a couple of weeks, but I finally decided to attend a youth service. And you know what? I absolutely hated it! I know that is harsh; but it is the truth. I hated it because I didn't know anyone, I felt out of place. But the thing I hated most, was when the instructors asked questions it always seems like they called on the quiet people the most. I didn't like to be called on. Needless to say, that was the first and last day I attended youth service. I also felt like I was getting nothing out of it. So I went back to the adult services and adult Bible studies, because I was learning. I felt like Jesus when he was a little boy sitting in the synagogues with the astute high priest. I didn't understand it then, but as I look back I realize that there was a purpose for me sitting under the mature teachings of my Pastor. God had given me the ability to chew the meat of the word at a young age. He had given me an understanding of the Word. He was maturing me for something. I am reminded of young David when the Prophet Samuel was instructed to go to Jesse's house and anoint one of his sons to be King of Israel. After Samuel went through seven sons and God denied them all, he called for the youngest of Jesse's sons. David was out tending the sheep. At a young age, God had David in the fields caring for the sheep, because one day he would have to shepherd God's chosen people. [1 Samuel 16:1-13]

Let me stop and say this to my readers. You may be at a place that you feel is way beyond what you are. But there is a purpose and a plan for your life. God has many of you right where He wants you. Because He is preparing you for what is to come.

The Beginning of the Journey

The Setup

Still on this journey of what's next, I started attending youth discipleship classes. It was a little uncomfortable at first, because I was still sour from my experience with the first youth service. But I enjoyed it. I began to actually talk to people and make friends. And I loved my teachers. I was actually learning in this class and they weren't just talking about sex and drugs and parties. We were working through different youth discipleship books learning about spiritual values for life. I enrolled in discipleship classes for a number of years. I never missed one session. If I was late, I was mad! I looked forward to getting to church on Monday nights. I loved all of my teachers because they knew how to relate and teach the young crowd. Since I was involved with discipleship, I was now in the loop of all the different youth events that were happening.

I began to get pulled in slowly, but surely. I would attend retreats and lock-ins. This was a big step for me. At about the age of 15, I really started getting serious. I was bored with what I was

doing. I now knew what salvation really meant --
that it was a relationship and not just a way out
of hell. God saved us from darkness because He
loves us, and so that we can be in communion
with Him. He desires that we have access to
everything He has. He wants to be connected
with us and be our Father. I learned that salvation
was a process and we had to continue to grow
and learn to strengthen our relationship with
God.

I ran across a term in my Christian journey called
Purpose. There were questions like "What is your
purpose?" "Why are you here?" "What does God
have designed for your life?" These questions put
a burden in my heart, because I didn't have an
answer. Like many of us I begin to wonder "Why
am I here?" I started the process of seeking out
my purpose. When I began to inquire of the Lord
what was my purpose He did not immediately
answer me, but allowed me to experience things
in my life which positioned me to meet my
purpose.

Chapter Two

Introduced to Purpose

Hello, my name is Jenice, what is yours? My name is Purpose; nice to finally meet you. The day I met purpose, it transformed my life completely. I will never forget the moment. In the previous chapter I mentioned I was involved with the Discipleship ministry. One day we were all sitting in class waiting for the stragglers to make it in and for the teachers to begin. We were talking and discussing our day. I happened to be at the front of the class sitting on the stool where the teacher would normally be. Before you knew it class began, the teachers were sitting in the seats along with the students and I was still at the front of the class. I couldn't move from that spot. The teachers began to review the lesson and before you knew it I was asking questions to the class. You would have thought I was the instructor. I had a good time that night.

Introduced to Purpose

The next week at teen church (yes, I started going) both of my discipleship instructors stopped me on my way into the classroom and said, "We noticed you looked very comfortable at the front of the class last week. We were wondering if you would like to be an Assistant Teacher?" Man, my face lit up and I had the biggest smile, because the Lord had answered my prayer. I gladly said YES!! It was like someone else inside of me spoke up before I could even process the thought. It was nothing but the Holy Spirit! At that moment the Holy Spirit inside of me was excited to see Purpose, because the Holy Spirit inside of me was ready to get to work, ready to complete His assignment in my life. He was ready for me to activate Him in a new way in my life. Of course, I knew that I had the Spirit of God in me, but I wasn't taking complete advantage of who He was and what He was capable of doing. It was just like Mary and her cousin Elisabeth. *And Mary arose in those days, and went into the hill country with haste, into a city of Judah; and entered into the house of Zacharias and saluted Elisabeth. And it came to pass, that, when Elisabeth heard the salutation of Mary the babe leaped in her womb; and Elisabeth was filled with the Holy Ghost, And she spoke out with a loud voice, and said, Blessed art thou among women, and blessed is the fruit of thy womb. And whence is this to me that the mother of my Lord should come to me? For, lo, as soon as the voice of the salutation sounded in mine ears, the babe leaped in my womb for joy. And blessed is she that believed: for there shall be a performance of those things which were told her from the Lord.* [Luke 1:39-45]

At that moment, something divine happened. When she heard the salutation, the babe leaped inside of her. John the Baptist was the babe inside of Elisabeth and Jesus was the babe inside of Mary. John the Baptist met his purpose, to prepare the way of Jesus Christ; to preach and baptize unto repentance. John was introduced to his purpose.

In my situation, my teachers represented Mary and they were spiritually carrying what I needed to begin my ministry. So when the Holy Spirit in me heard the voice of purpose; He leaped on the inside of me and answered before I could think about it.

I began to teach alongside my adult teachers and it was very fulfilling. Something great was happening to me. I began noticing this boldness that I had when it came to teaching. I loved what the Lord was doing in and through me. The fact that I was able to teach my peers in a way that they could understand, the fact I could read the Word and have a clear understanding of it and teach it to others. The Lord was truly at work in my life. I thought that it was just for me; that I was fulfilling the purpose for my life. I was, but it didn't stop there.

Shortly after that other people began to see a call on my life. The Youth Pastor, at the time, Pastor Bryan White began referring to me as "preacher". He saw the gift to preach on my life. But imagine how I felt. I was like "Oh No", because I remembered the vision I had when I was 13. I still had not mentioned it to anyone. But I started getting invitations to

preach at retreats and revivals and conferences.
God was enlarging my territory. Before I knew it,
preaching became my love! I preached my first
youth revival at my home church and the topic
was "What's the Holdup? Time to Push". I will
never forget that message. I was so nervous, but
it was such a powerful word and powerful
delivery. That was the day I said, "This is what I
was born to do". It was similar to what I saw in
that vision when I was 13. I cannot describe the
feeling I had. Of course, I was nervous, I had
butterflies in my stomach the entire day and
especially while I was in the back room waiting to
come out into the service. I will never forget it.
Pastor Keean Sutton introduced me and it was
time for me to stand and preach the word
before this large congregation, with some of my
family members there.

I don't know what happened but words started
rolling off of my tongue. Before I knew it the Holy
Spirit took full control. It was like a total
transformation took place. It was another time in
my life when God was at work in my life, because
there is no way Jenice would be standing in

front of people talking the way I was talking. I began to slowly but surely accept that call on my life, but I wasn't in any rush. People were trying to "encourage" me to talk to my pastor and get licensed, but I knew it wasn't my time. I needed to be developed and mentored. A lot of my male friends were entering the ministry, but I wasn't one to follow the crowd. I moved when God said to move. I waited and prayed and waited. I was comfortable with what I was doing. There was no need to get licensed since God had already opened some doors for me. My name was getting around to different churches, the invitations were coming in, so I was good. I preached because I loved it. I didn't want any recognition, and I didn't want the responsibility of being a minister.

I toiled with it for a long time; I even started running from it. I always say when you find yourself running from God; you will end up running right into Him. In other words you can't run from him nor can you hide? [Psalms 139]

Introduced to Purpose

During this time I was learning more about myself and who I was in Christ. I always wanted more, because I knew there was more to God. I was introduced to a youth ministry that was started by a few radical young men, called Vigor Youth Ministry. I was approached by the leader of the ministry, Pastor Keean Sutton. He was very passionate about the vision he received from the Lord. He was determined to turn the hearts of young people back to God and to train leaders to be effective in their communities, churches and businesses.

I began attending their meetings and soon became a member of the ministry. Prayer nights, conferences, retreats and ministry meetings were my extracurricular activities. My relationship with the Lord was getting stronger. I was learning more about myself and my spiritual gifts. I was soon appointed to the position of Assistant Director. I did not know how I was appointed to this position, nor did I feel I was capable of doing it, but I figured I could put to use what I was learning in college.

Introduced to Purpose

I served in Vigor for three years before I was on to my next assignment. It is never an easy task to leave a ministry you've given your all too. However, it was time and I moved on to the Missions Ministry at my church where I served under my uncle, Pastor Arnold Davis. I had an opportunity to go on foreign mission trips where I learned so much about evangelism and sharing my faith with the world. I assisted the Mission Ministry with developing a youth missions group.

Can you see the pieces of the puzzle being put together? God has a plan for all of our lives and each season of your life is another piece of the puzzle that fits into your final destiny. God puts us in different places to equip us and shape our character so that we are able to stand and complete what He has for us. This is why it is so important that we are willing to go through the process and not try to go around what God is doing in our lives. We should be obedient and trust Him instead of having to learn the same lessons over and over again. Of course, this is not always the case. Our flesh gets in the way. We try to do things on our own, only to mess things up and have to do it the way the Lord originally planned.

The Lord put this burning in my heart to preach and I finally harkened to His call into ministry. I went to my youth pastor, Pastor White and said, "I have been praying and I am ready". Pastor White had the biggest smile on his face. He gave me a hug and said "Alright we will set up a meeting Pastor Sheals."

One Sunday after service Pastor White took me up to Pastor's study. We walked in and my Pastor was sitting behind his desk. He took one look at me and without me saying a word, he said "How long have you been called baby?" I replied a long time. He told me to set up a meeting with him for the coming week; which I did. The time came for the meeting and I was very nervous, but all went well. Pastor White attended the meeting with me and Pastor Sheals began to impart wisdom into me. He placed me in the wilderness where I would fast and pray about the call on my life. It was only suppose to be for seven months, but I stayed for a year. I wanted to make sure I heard the voice of the Lord. During this time, I started attending Ministers in Training classes at the church. Before you knew it I was scheduled to preach my initial sermon to be licensed as a minister. Wow!! This was crazy. Look where the Lord brought me from. I was on a journey for Christ, to be used by the Lord to preach and teach the Gospel.

Being a minister is not about having a title, wearing a robe or sitting on the pulpit. When you look at the many definitions for the word minister, it breaks down to one simple word -- servant. Preaching sermons is just a piece of the pie, but the responsibilities extend far and beyond the pulpit. Ministers must serve as Christ served and ministered. Jesus spoke to his disciples and stated, *But so shall it not be among you; but whosoever will be great among you, shall be your minister; And whosoever of you will be the chiefest, shall be servant of all. For even the Son of man came not to be ministered unto, but to minister, and to give his life a ransom for many.* [Mark 10:43-45]

Introduced to Purpose

Ministers have to be willing to get down in the trenches, roll up your sleeves and get dirty. You have a responsibility to visit the sick and shut in, go to the hospitals and speak words of encouragement to those who are infirmed and minister to the widows and orphans. But the ultimate responsibility is to do the work of an evangelist. As a minister of the gospel the top priority is to share the gospel with a lost and dying world. The Apostle Paul wrote, *How then shall they call on him in whom they have not believed? And how shall they believe in him of whom they have not heard? And how shall they hear without a preacher? And how shall they preach, except they be sent? As it is written, how beautiful are the feet of them that preach the gospel of peach and bring glad tidings of good things!* [Romans 10:14-15]

Sharing the good news is not just a responsibility for a clergy minister, but it is for every lay person, every believer. Jesus admonished us in the scriptures to *Go therefore, and teach all nations, baptizing them in the name of the Father, and of the Son, and of the Holy Ghost:*

Introduced to Purpose

Teaching them to observe all things whatsoever I have commanded you: and, lo, I am with you always, even unto the end of the world. [Matthew 28:19-20]

So you see when you really dissect the responsibilities of a minister, it is in no way a glamorous position. It is a position in which one must remain humble to ensure that everything that is done is done unto the glory of the Lord. Although this is not as attractive, it is so rewarding spiritually. Now that I have been introduced to purpose, let's see what I have encountered on this journey.

Chapter Three

Who Are You Accountable To? (Spiritual Mentors)

My favorite letters in the Bible are the letters that the Apostle Paul wrote to his young protégé Timothy. These letters are filled with wisdom and experience. Paul took young Timothy under his wings and mentored him. He told Timothy the things that he would experience in ministry and how to deal with issues that would arise. I love the relationship that these two had. I can only imagine that Timothy truly loved and looked up to Paul.

During the years that I struggled with my call, there were not many female ministers on TV. Nor were there any that seemed to connect with my spirit. One day a friend of mine brought this tape to my house called No More Sheets. A group of us sat down and watched this VHS. I was astounded by the female preacher. I couldn't relate to what she was preaching about, but what captured me was the type of delivery she had. It was one of power and boldness.

Who Are You Accountable To?

I was captivated by that and I felt a strong liking for her ministry. I watched her when she was on TV and listened to more of her tapes. There was something about her style of delivery that connected with me. I was looking for an example of how women should behave in ministry.

During this time, women in my church were just coming into their own. It had only been a couple of years since my Pastor began to license female ministers. At that time, the female ministers were classified as Evangelists. They didn't wear robes, nor did they sit in the pulpit. They would sit on the front pew and dress in the same colors to show unity. It was not long before the front row was filled with women. Some of these women had the call on their lives for years, but as I found out later, because of the timing and traditions they were not accepted to hold the title of a minister and preach in the church.

Who Are You Accountable To?

There was a big transition happening in the body of Christ, as more women were joining the ministry and some were even becoming Pastors. I remember hearing horror stories of people that did not accept or approve woman preachers. I was thinking, "Great, what a time to be called into the ministry!" One day I remember saying "Nope, this is not for me."

I decided to attend a women's conference at a major church in the Atlanta area. I went alone and there was so much traffic. I saw protesters standing outside with their large posters yelling and chanting against women preachers. Some of the signs had scriptures on them defending their evil objections. I was trying to drive and listen to what they are yelling, as well as trying to write down some of the scriptures. It was a mess! The church was so crowded that I ended up in the overflow. After about 10 minutes I left and went home. On the ride home I was thinking about those protesters and the looks on their faces. I was done; I decided this is not for me. I don't need to become as licensed minister, I am good with how things are going. When I got home I called a friend to tell them about the experience I just had.

Who Are You Accountable To?

Later that night I looked up all scriptures I managed to write down while I was driving. I wasn't even a licensed minister yet and just the fact that I was called was a great struggle for me. I was conflicted about whether or not this was the true purpose for my life.

When I was growing up my dream was to play basketball, go overseas and make some money. This was way before the ABL and WNBA. But we see what happened. I gave up basketball and the overseas work I was doing was missions work. After all that I became a preacher. The Lord certainly does have a sense of humor. Not only does He have a sense of humor, but He has a plan and a purpose for each of us. It is up to us to seek Him for what it is.

It is a wonderful feeling to know your purpose in life, because you have a reason to live and you have something to reach towards. When you talk to people who have not sought God for their purpose, they will tell you they don't know why they are here. They feel lost because they don't feel like they are fulfilling their purpose. Nothing is satisfying for them. Often these are the people that one day you see them doing this and the next day you see them doing that, bouncing from one profession to the other. But when you have a purpose you are focused and you are able to develop goals to strive for. Perhaps it gives you a little more stability in life. I admonish you to take time to ask God what you are purposed to do here on earth. He will tell you. I am a living witness that He will.

I began hearing my male friends throwing around the term "Spiritual Fathers". I was wondering to myself, "Wow they have men in their lives they can go to for advice in ministry and mentor them!" I knew that my Pastor was my spiritual leader, but there was no way that I could get a one on one type of bond with him to grow in ministry the way I desired. I thought, if there are spiritual fathers there have to be spiritual mothers. I was now on a quest. I was looking for a woman that was in ministry that could mentor me. As female preachers began to burst on the scene in my church there was always one woman in particular that stood out to me. I would always remember watching her -- the way she dressed, how she praised the Lord, just her overall mannerisms.

Who Are You Accountable To?

I did not know her name until sometime later, I found out that she was the mother of a friend. There was something about this lady that connected with me.

As I said earlier I was a shy kid, but I was always very observant. During the time I wasn't involved in the Teen Ministry but sat in the main services with all of my family, I would watch this lady from afar. When we had to walk around for tithes and offering, I would try to get a good look at her with my serious face and maybe gently smile. Some of my friends that had encounters with her, knew of her and the powerful ministry she had, so I heard things here and there. I began to develop a far off respect for her and there was something in me that knew this lady would be a big part of my spiritual growth.

Later that year, I was chosen to be the speaker at our annual youth day program. I was ecstatic. It was also so amazing because I was just getting back into the United States. I had been out of the country on my first missionary journey to Haiti. That trip was a life changing experience and was the boost that helped me preach a powerful message. The topic of this sermon was "Harden not your heart". It was a convicting message, and the Holy Spirit really used me as many people came to Christ that day.

After that day, many women came to me wanting to be my mentor. They gave me their numbers, but they just did not feel right in my spirit. I used to work at my church's school as an assistant and I also worked at the afterschool program. Every day I would always see this lady pick up her son from the afterschool program. Finally, one day after a chapel service I saw her and said to myself, "I have to talk to her". I was at a point when I was thinking about it all the time, wondering what I was going to say. I was about to walk out of the church headed to my class and there she was; right at the exit I had to walk through. See how the Lord will set up opportunities for you. I saw her talking to someone, and I waited in the distance until the opportune time. I walked up to her with my hands in my pockets. I believe I hugged her and said, "Can I talk to you?" She had this warm smile on her face and said, "Sure". We walked over to

the side and I began to tell her about all these
people who were coming to me asking to be my
mentor. I had been hearing about spiritual
fathers, and I need a spiritual mother. I asked her
if she would be my spiritual mother, because
there was something about her that was
connecting me to her. I told her how God spoke
her name so plainly to me. With tears swelling up
in her eyes, Pastor Veta Blanding said "I would be
honored". I released a big sigh of relief inside me,
even though I knew she would say yes, because
it was ordained by God. She prayed with me,
hugged me and gave me her number and told
me to call her. I was so happy that I had finally
done it. I now had a spiritual mother and a
mentor. It was really a big moment in my life.

Who are you accountable to?

Building a Relationship

God is our Father. It is not enough for us to become born again or "saved", we must build a relationship with the Lord. There are many ways to get to know God. One way to know God is through reading and studying the Bible. By reading the Bible we get to understand who God is, what He desires from us as His children and how we should live our lives so it is pleasing to Him. Another way to build a relationship with the Lord is to spend time in prayer. Through prayer you speak to the Lord and He speaks back to you. Prayer is two way communication. Yes, we oft get this confused. We pray to God complaining about what we do not have and what we want Him to give us and then say Amen. This is such a wrong way to approach prayer. It is important that we reverence God, confess our sins, intercede for others, and then make our petition unto Him.

Who are you accountable to?

Don't just end the prayer, sit for a moment and allow God time to share with you. I believe many times we lose out on God and His instructions because we are in such a hurry. The next time you pray take some time to listen before you say Amen.

Another way we can build a relationship with the Lord is through praise and worship. The Lord responds to praise and worship. During intimate moments of worship, God will reveal Himself to you in many different ways, because you have set aside time to be in His presence. What better way is there to get to know God, than to spend quality time with Him. As I stated previously, God is our Father, and He is the one we should go to and consult with. However, God has also placed people in our lives for reasons and seasons, and He places some people in our lives to whom we can look up to and get advice from. When you look throughout the Bible you see mentors and mentees Eli and Samuel, Elijah and Elisha, Saul and David. In this same reference you must build a relationship with those who cover you.

Who are you accountable to?

The first step was when I approached my mentor. The second step was for the two of us to get to know each other. This went beyond a phone call here and there, but going out to lunch, being invited over to her home and being welcomed into her family. By communicating with each other she was able to see me as an individual and pour into me the wisdom and knowledge I needed to better myself as an individual and as a preacher. I recall the time she invited me to her women's conference "Women in Ministry." This particular conference was held in Decatur, Florida. I was the only young person there; 17 at the time. I was still very timid and Pastor Blanding and I were just getting to know one another. I felt very awkward being the youngest there, but I made it through the weekend and I had a great time. On our way back home I decided to go sit with her and have a conversation. This one conversation caused such a change in my life. We made small talk, and I began telling her where I was from, how I grew up and what the Lord was doing in me. But she had already seen a lot of herself in me and she began to tell me things that only I knew. I broke down and began to cry. If you know me, you would know that I do not show much emotion. I've always had a hard exterior, but she broke right threw it with a few simple words and the great amount of motherly love that oozes out of her spirit. I knew at that point, she would be a major part of my life for the rest of my life.

There are many people in my life that were instrumental in shaping me into the person I am today. But Pastor Blanding was the person I needed in my life at that time, because she was first a woman, second she was active in ministry, and third she was the founder of her own ministry. This was the direction I knew God was calling me to. God makes no mistakes. When you ask the Father for something, He will give it to you in His time, and trust me He knows best. He knew exactly whose wings to sit me under. He knew the person that would be able to birth me out spiritually.

Who are you accountable to?

Another individual that played a major part in shaping me in ministry was my uncle, Pastor Arnold Davis. The blessing about my uncle is that I had the opportunity to witness where he came from to where God elevated him to. My uncle wasn't always a saved man. He grew up in the hard streets of New York and did things that today he can give his testimony of how God delivered him. I have seen the transformation in him going from a man of the streets to a deacon to a minister and now to a pastor. He has always been an influence in my life. Because I grew up without my father, he was one of my father figures. When he became a minster, he began to work with Missions and Outreach and this became his love. My uncle will tell you he doesn't need a pulpit, he would rather be out in the bush somewhere preaching the gospel and loving on God's people. He has been to many different countries spreading the Gospel of Jesus Christ: Africa, Haiti, Thailand, Jamaica, and India just to name a few. He was the one who actually introduced me to Missions and I began to work with him in developing a youth track. I had the opportunity to go to Haiti and Jamaica with him.

Who are you accountable to?

Under his leadership I have learned so much. I learned how to care for people, regardless of the state they are in. I have learned what the true church really looks like and how it should operate. I have learned what pure ministry is. Because of his example, I have a burden for people and a burden to travel this world and share the love and gospel of Jesus Christ.

There are many others who played a vital role in me being the woman I am today. However, I chose to use these individuals as my examples of spiritual mentorship. These individuals are still in my life, and they continue to encourage me, love me, support me and correct me. Much of who I am and where I am I attribute to them. While you are reading this you may be in a place where you need a mentor. My suggestion to you is to sincerely pray to God about it, listen for His instructions and be obedient. He will bring people in your life or lead you to someone that will encourage you, as well as be truthful with you.

Who are you accountable to?

Accepting Correction

Who likes to admit they are wrong? Who likes to be wrong? Not many people, but it is important to have people in your life who challenge you and push you to be a better individual. The word of God says, *Whom the Lord loveth he chasteneth*, [Hebrews 12:6]. As spiritual children, it is important that we are accounted for and that we be willing to take a rebuke. Let's face it, we all mess up and sometimes make crazy decisions. As spiritual children we must submit and respect the word of those who are in authority over us.

A spiritual mentor is like a parent, caring for you, protecting you, and keeping watch for your soul. Let us take a look at the Biblical example of Eli and Samuel. When Samuel was a little boy before he became a prophet; he sat under the leadership and teaching of the priest Eli. Samuel's mother Hannah dedicated Samuel when he was a baby back to the Lord and she told the Lord that as long as Samuel was alive he was lent to Him.

Who are you accountable to?

Samuel grew up and ministered unto the Lord under the care of Eli. There was a time when the Lord came to speak to Samuel. Samuel did not yet know the voice of the Lord so he went to Eli. After the third time, Eli perceived it was the Lord that was calling the young boy and Eli instructed Samuel to say "Speak Lord, thy servant heareth." What I learned from this part of the story is that there are times that we as children walk into and encounter things that are unfamiliar to us as Samuel did. He went to his spiritual father. It was Eli who taught Samuel whose voice he was hearing and how to respond to it. We, like Samuel, must have people in our lives who we can go to and seek counsel. Eli was familiar with the voice of God and could mentor young Samuel. That is the purpose of spiritual mentors to help us with areas of life that are unusual to us, but proverbial to them. As I stated before, God is our ultimate source, but He will place others in our lives to be examples for us.

Who are you accountable to?

Please understand that in no way should our spiritual mentors take the place of God in our lives. They are merely God-sent individuals that have experience in secular and spiritual matters that can aid and assist us in our journey. Don't fall into a trap that so many people do out of ignorance and the influence of the enemy by making their leaders gods. I see this so much in Christendom. People begin to follow the man or woman of God instead of the God in them. When this happens individuals put the word of man over the Word of God. Their focus is on building a relationship with man rather than developing their relationship with God. I have talked to many people about decisions they are trying to make or having a conversation about spiritual matters and all they continue to say is, pastor said this, minister told me this, prophet spoke this. But my question is, WHAT DID GOD SAY? Too many people get caught up on what their leaders are saying and not confirming it with the Bible and not seeking God.

Who are you accountable to?

This is a very dangerous place to be, not just for the individual, but for the leader who is well aware but not putting a stop to it. He or she is getting a high off of the popularity. This is a huge problem in the Body of Christ when no one is holding our leaders accountable for their actions. The first commandment is *thou shalt have no other god before me.* [Exodus 20:3]. Our God is a very jealous God and He will not share His Glory with anyone. If you find that you have been worshiping your leaders instead of God, then you need to go to Him and repent. And if you are a leader who allows yourself to continually take the credit for what God is doing, then please go to God and repent. It is fine for us to admire people, but to be consumed with a person and to strive hard to be more like them than Jesus Christ puts us in a danger zone.

Who are you accountable to?

We are all fearfully and wonderfully made, [Psalms 139:14] God has created each of us with a unique identity. There are billions of people on this earth and you will find no one with your identity. No one has your DNA and no one has your same fingerprint. We have to be extremely careful that we do not lose who we are in ministry or in anything that we do. Too many times people get caught up running after their leaders trying to gain cool points, and in the process lose themselves. Instead of walking in the gifts and the calling God created for them, some people take on the leader's identity and become a spiritual clone. As a result you are forfeiting the ability for God to really use you in the purpose and plan He has designed for you. I strongly believe that if you sit underneath a person long enough you will begin to take on some of their characteristics. You might find yourself saying some of the things they say, making some of the movements they make, because you have been exposed to their style of teaching and preaching for so long.

Who are you accountable to?

One Sunday my pastor, Pastor Noble Williams of Greater Mount Zion Baptist Church in Phenix City, Alabama asked me to preach at the second service, because he was going to be on vacation. When my Pastor gets excited in the spirit he does three things that stand out. One is that he starts kicking his right leg back and forth. He will also yell to the congregation "Say yeah" and the other thing is he will ask "Is there anybody here?" I was preaching and got caught up in the moment and said "Is there anybody here?" I caught myself! I was laughing on the inside and said "Oh Lord, that is Pastor Williams coming out of me". It's okay for things like that to happen, because that is my spiritual father and I have taken on some of his characteristics. However, this does not mean I should become my leader's duplicate. It vexes me when I see young men and women coming up in ministry and they are tagging along on the coat tails of others, dressing like them, trying hard to pray like them and preach like them. Stop! Be yourself and be who God created you to be. It is so disturbing when a person who has the gift of teaching, forces themselves to, as we say in the church "hoop and holler" like their pastor does. It is not only an embarrassment to you, but it is a bad reflection on the church and its leadership. If you get nothing else from all that you read, remember to be yourself and allow the Holy Spirit to work through you the way He desires to. I tell young people all the time, no matter how much they look up to me, "I am not perfect, I am still working out my own soul salvation just like everyone else and I am who God has created me to be, so be who God has created you to be." I try to teach individuals how to seek God for their purpose and be comfortable in their own skin. I have seen many ministries destroyed because they went with a stolen identity. But thanks to God He is a forgiving and patient God. Through the Holy Spirit, He will bring things to your attention and take you through a deprogramming process to strip you of all the things you are not, to get you to the core of who He created you to be.

Who are you accountable to?

The leaders in our lives are under shepherds as they follow the leadership of The Shepherd, Jesus Christ. They have a responsibility to oversee, teach us the word of God, encourage and correct us. However they are not to control us. God gave us all something called "free will". He gives us the ability to choose. I absolutely hurt when I see a young person make a wrong decision and head down the wrong path. Nevertheless, that young person has the right to make the decisions they make. As the leader, I can only encourage, share the correct path to take and pray for them. I cannot make someone do what I know is the right thing for them to do. I have to trust that the Word of God has been planted and that the Holy Spirit will work in their life. As a leader I cannot intimidate, dominate or manipulate those that God has placed in my care. It is wrong and not a reflection of God, but a reflection of Satan. If you find yourself in a church where this is taking place, talk to the Lord and follow His guiding. If you are a leader and you find yourself reflecting these attributes, it is time to look in the mirror and go to God for forgiveness and restoration.

Who are you accountable to?

This is why it is important to have someone in your life that is going to tell you the truth. Sometimes the truth hurts. But I would much rather be around people who are going to tell me the truth and hurt my feelings for a moment, than to be surrounded by people who agree with everything I say and be hurt for a lifetime. I thank God for surrounding me with great mentors and great friends.

I have been told that I am very stubborn, but I can say that I am pretty good at being obedient when I am told something. Especially when I know that it is for my good. There have been times when I was about to make or made some ignorant decisions and when I sought out counsel, I was corrected not just by my mentors, but by God. When a spiritual parent or mentor is connected with God they know how to correct you and encourage you. Encouragement is so important. As a spiritual mentor you want to teach your mentee how to recover and learn from bad decisions. You want to push them to continue making wise decisions. Another important aspect of being a spiritual mentor is to share your past experiences. This will help your mentee not to make the same foolish mistakes.

There were some times in ministry when I had no idea what I was doing, but ignorantly worked my way through. It wasn't until I had someone sit and teach me the correct way. A perfect example is when I was just coming into the knowledge of demonic influences, oppressions and possessions. One day I attended a youth service and during the praise and worship service demons began to manifest in a few individuals. This was the first time I had ever witnessed anything like that in my life. The closest thing I had seen was from the movie "The Exorcist." Half of the people there, including me, had no clue or experience on casting out demons. There we were -- fifty of us yelling at these poor people, fighting with the demons. By the end of the night we were all physically and spiritually drained. I look back now and laugh, but trust me it wasn't funny then. I remember being frustrated and confused, thinking that I didn't have the power that Jesus spoke about in the scriptures, the power to cast out devils. *And he ordained twelve, that they*

Who are you accountable to?

should be with him, and that he might send them forth to preach, And to have power to heal sicknesses, and to cast out devils:[Mark 3:14-15] It wasn't that I didn't have the power, I had to learn how to use it correctly. This was something I had to be taught. It was only by the grace of God that none of us were hurt. God knew our heart. If we didn't know anything else; we knew how to say the name Jesus. I thank God for wisdom and growth. We, as spiritual children, must be willing and open to correction and instruction. It will only help make us better and stronger individuals to accomplish the purpose that God has placed in our lives. There are going to be times when your feelings get hurt by your spiritual parents. Don't take it personal, but realize there is a purpose behind the correction. If you are yoked up with someone that is not correcting you, but always praising you, maybe it is time for you to re-evaluate.

Chapter Four

Too Young

Many times when you ask young people why they have not given their life completely to the Lord, you often hear the excuse "I am too young". I say you are never too young. I was nine years old when I became born again and 15 years old when I really decided that I was going to go all out for the Lord and fulfill His purpose for my life. I have been going ever since. I have been asked,"Why did you make such a commitment at a young age?" and I ask "Why not". At times it has been very challenging, but the blessings that I have received as a result of my decision are indescribable.

When I was about 17, I wrote this song. I was inspired because my peers did not understand why I made the choices that I made.

Too Young

"They want to know why I do what I do.
They want to know why I had to finish school.
They want to know why I didn't pay ball.
They want to know why my standards are so tall,
They want to know why I spent all my days at
work half the day in the house and the rest at
church."

Since I never finished the song "They want to
know", I'll give you my response now. The reason
why is because I owe God my life. I am here and
have what I have because God made it
possible. I do what I do because God chose me!
Many are called but few are chosen. [Matthew
22:14]. I often asked God the question, "Why
me?" This is something you may even ask
yourself. The reason He chose you and me is
because He trusts us with the purpose He has
placed in us. All that our heavenly Father has
given us is precious and He will not just give you a
gift and then leave you by yourself. He equips us
and has given us the Holy Spirit to guide and
teach us. However, we have a responsibility in
this relationship with the Lord. We must be willing

to seek after Him and ask for direction concerning our lives. God wants to be totally included in our lives. I can honestly say I loved and enjoyed serving the Lord as a youth. Many people used to tell me, "I wish I had started working for the Lord at your age, because I would be so much further in ministry". It really is the truth, when you make the decision to work for the Lord at a young age, He will elevate you beyond measure.

There are many great men in the Bible that began serving the Lord and working for His kingdom at a young age. Joshua is one of my favorite people in the Bible. Joshua was a young man who served under a great leader - Moses. There was something about Joshua that made him stand out among his peers. *The Lord said to Moses, take Joshua son of Nun, a man in whom is the spirit, and lay your hand upon him; And set him before Eleazar the priest and all the congregation and give him a charge in their sight. And put some of your honor and authority upon him, that all the congregation of Israelites may obey him.* [Numbers 27:18-20]. Joshua stood out because he had the spirit of the Lord in him. Joshua understood what it meant to walk with God and to stay in His presence. *And the LORD spake unto Moses face to face, as a man speaketh unto his friend. And he turned again into the camp: but his servant Joshua, the son of Nun, a young man, departed not out of the tabernacle.* [Exodus 33:11].

God trusted Joshua and knew that he would be able to lead the children of Israel. Joshua was faithful over little and God rewarded him with much. When Moses sent the twelve spies over into Canaan to survey the land, the young boys Joshua and his homeboy Caleb came back with the report that we can take the enemy. Joshua saw things through the eyes of God and because he stayed in the presence of God he had a connection that could not be broken, regardless of what came against him. God was so pleased with Joshua and Caleb; they were the only two spies that were allowed to enter the Promised Land. *Surely none of the men that came up out of Egypt, from twenty years old and upward, shall see the land which I swear unto*

Too Young

Abraham, unto Isaac, and unto Jacob; because they have not wholly followed me: Save Caleb the son of Jephunneh the Kenezite, and Joshua the son of Nun: for they have wholly followed the LORD. [Numbers 32:11]

When you are faithful over a few things, God will reward you with much. [Matthew 25:23] God is looking for young people who will stay in His presence, who He can fill with the power of the Holy Spirit to do great things for the Kingdom. I can honestly say that if I could go back in time, the only thing I would change is starting earlier. I do not regret at all the decision I made to serve God at a young age. I think people misjudge being sold out to the Lord. I believe many people feel they will be missing out on life and fun, but the truth of the matter is this journey with the Lord is an invigorating adventure. There are so many endless possibilities with the Lord and the blessings that come along with serving Him are unreal. All I can say is try it. The word of the Lord declares, *My son, forget not my law; but let thine heart keep my commandments: For length of days, and long life, and peace, shall they add to thee.* [Proverbs 3:1-2]

Too Young

I am so happy that I am one of His chosen
children. He sees more in me than anyone can
see, and He trusts me enough to give me vision
and blessings. It is awesome! Now I do have to
share that everything is not always peaches and
cream. There were many times, when I did not
feel worthy to be who God made me. I wanted
out, I didn't want to be a minister any more. I
didn't want to have the gifts and the talents I
had been blessed with. I just wanted to be an
ordinary person, live a regular life like everyone
else and not have the responsibility of being a
leader.

Growing up I would see all my friends and kids in
school and in the neighborhood doing what they
wanted to do -- going out, partying, having
relationships, living a typical teenage life style.
But I was doing what I needed to do in order to
grow spiritually and not be in any type of
situation that would compromise my anointing.
Yes, this was the decision I made but it was not
always an easy choice. I knew that salvation was
free, but the anointing costs and I had to be

willing to pay the price to get all that I could from the Lord. I am still reaching for more of God.

I was never a bad child. I never got into any trouble and for some reason, not on my own merit, I made wise decisions. There was something in me since I was a little child that wanted to please God. There were times that I felt like I was missing out on things and I shouldn't have committed to God like I did. However, there is a love that I have for God that outweighed those negative thoughts. The love I have for Him keeps me going during the toughest times. When you have a love and a passion for purpose, you won't give up on God -- you cannot give up on God. . . . *the gifts and the call are without repentance.* [Romans 11:29] God didn't give you gifts so that you could give them back to Him and walk away. He gave you gifts and talents so that you can give Him the glory through it.

Too Young

God you want me to do what?

In the summer of 2002 I turned 21 years old. I felt I was already doing enough for the Lord. I was at church three to four times a week either teaching, in class or in a planning meeting. This was before I learned how to say "no." I was sitting at home watching television and working on the computer when I got up to take out the trash. As I was walking to the dumpster, I heard the Lord say "I want you to start a ministry." Trust me when I say, it shocked me and threw me for a loop. I stopped in my tracks and said "I can't do that." I started walking again and He said, "Yes you can". This really startled me. I didn't know what to say didn't know who to tell and didn't know where to begin. When I came back inside, I went to my room, sat down and said, "God you want me to do what?" I really believe God was laughing at me. It took about two weeks to get over the fact that God wanted me to do something of this magnitude.

Too Young

Getting over my initial fear took some time, but I remember ideas started coming to me so clearly. My mind was just working a mile a minute. When He gave me the name and vision and purpose of the ministry, all I could do was write as fast as I could. This was during the time I was in the wilderness waiting to have my follow up meeting with my pastor. I went to my mentor and shared with her all that I had written down and what the Lord had given me. She listened intently and read my brochure. She admonished me to talk to church leadership. I followed her counsel and first spoke to the Assistant Pastor, and then to the Senior Pastor. They both gave me sound wisdom and advice on starting a ministry. I began a small Bible Study with about 10 participants. Over the years the vision expanded. I did all of the legal paperwork to have the ministry incorporated and to become a non-profit organization. God gave me more and more ideas, much of it I couldn't share with anyone because it wasn't time. God knew that I wasn't going to be able to take everyone along with me on this journey.

Too Young

About a year and half later, after we had been conducting Bible Studies on a regular basis, the Lord told me to shut it down. I did so out of obedience but I went through a very tough season in my life. I felt like a failure. The ministry wasn't going as I thought it should have -- we were not doing anything. I kept thinking, "I told you God, I couldn't do it." This was a huge struggle and I was very disappointed. I didn't feel that I was capable of leading, so I shied away from taking on any leadership roles. But the more I tried to stay in the background, the more God sent opportunities my way. It was driving me crazy! I didn't understand why the Lord was trying to entrust me with even more, when I felt like I had failed Him. I was being approached by person after person, ministry after ministry.

I was even being approached by ministries outside of my church. I couldn't believe it. It was kind of overwhelming, but regardless of what I felt or how much I thought I wasn't capable, I had to be obedient to the Lord. I did not understand it then, but as I look back now I see why the Lord took me through that. He knew that if I stayed in the background I would never overcome that disappointment and be able to experience the successes He has favored me to accomplish. Every season in your life is to prepare you for the next. God has to build our character to enable us to handle the next level He desires to take us to. If I never experienced the different phases that I went through, I would not know what I know now. Begin to treasure every season in your life, because it is ultimately for a bigger purpose which is to bring greater glory to the Father.

Choices (Church or Club)

Peer pressure is a part of life, whether you are young or old. The pressures from others around you will always be there. I recall a time in my life when friends of mine, who were Christians, tried to get me to go to the club. I had never been to a club before and the idea crossed my mind once or twice just out of curiosity. Ultimately I didn't have a desire to go and felt that I would compromise all that I believed in and taught others. These friends didn't understand where I was coming from when I turned the offer down. "It is fun, there's nothing wrong with going to the club and dancing, you don't have to drink, and you're not going to hell." These were all the comments I heard to coerce me into going, but I stood my ground and I am glad that I did.

Now this is my opinion and you can agree with me or not, but I don't feel that a worldly club is a place for a Christian to be.

Too Young

In scripture the Apostle Paul admonishes us, *I beseech you therefore, brethren, by the mercies of God, that ye present your bodies a living sacrifice, holy, acceptable unto God, [which is] your reasonable service. And be not conformed to this world: but be ye transformed by the renewing of your mind, that ye may prove what [is] that good, and acceptable, and perfect, will of God.* [Romans 12:1-2] Why would I confess to being a light and go to the club and represent the darkness of the world? *Love not the world, neither the things [that are] in the world. If any man love the world, the love of the Father is not in him. For all that [is] in the world, the lust of the flesh, and the lust of the eyes, and the pride of life, is not of the Father, but is of the world.* [1 John 2:15-16]

Now, if you are going to the clubs to witness and pass out tracks -- then go for it. But I seriously doubt the majority of the people reading this will go to a club for those reasons. My point is that we cannot profess to be a light for Jesus and then put it out when we want to. There is nothing in a club that is glorifying God. Nothing in that club is going to make a person say "Wow I want to live for Christ". We cannot witness to the world about being a Christian and do the same thing that the world is doing. There has to be a standard, and you have to be willing to stand out and be different from the crowd. I hear what you are saying, "But life is so boring. What am I going to do to have fun?" Believe me when I tell you, life is full of possibilities and exciting things to do. Don't place yourself in situations and places that will compromise your relationship with God, and cause another brother or sister in Christ to stumble.

The lessons I learned during that time of my life was the importance of maintaining a standard. It is so important in life to have standards and not allow anyone to provoke you to lower those standards for any reason. As a child of God, our standard should be Holiness. We should measure our life according to the Word of God. The question we should ask ourselves often is, "Am I making the Father proud of me by doing what I'm doing?" This is something I ask myself before getting involved with anything. It helps me to be accountable. The fact that I've stood strong on what I believed and professed, and because I did not allow anyone to break the standard I set for my life, God has used my life as an example to those same friends. They saw I was not going to back down and they respected me for that reason. Never again did they ask me to do anything that would compromise my relationship with God. It is not only about what we say, but our lifestyle is a witness. People pay more attention to how you behave than what you say. Let your lifestyle be a witness for Jesus Christ. *But be ye doers of the word, and not hearers only, deceiving your own selves.* [James 1:22]

Choices are a big part of our everyday life. Will we always make the correct choice? No, we will not. However it is important to follow the guidance of the Holy Spirit and repent when we do wrong. God is truly faithful and just to forgive us of our sins. Even though we will not always make the correct choices, here are some keys that will help aid in making healthier choices:

1) Submit your will to the Lord, 2) Involve God in every aspect of your life, and 3) Daily crucify your flesh and renew your mind.

The first key is to submit our will to the Father's will. Even Jesus knew the importance of this principle. Although Jesus was divinity, He was at the same time human. The Lord knew that if He didn't submit to the Father's will, He would not be able to go through what He was about to endure. *Saying, Father, if thou be willing, remove this cup from me: nevertheless not my will, but thine, be done.* [Luke 22:42] Jesus abhorred His crucifixion and the physical torture He would endure, and He expressed to God what He was feeling. Knowing that His death would bring forgiveness and salvation to mankind, He put aside His will. When we submit our will to the Father, it is a expression of dependency and trust.

The second key is to include God in every aspect of your life. God desires to be involved in our lives, it shows the Father that we are concerned about what He thinks. God isn't just interested in being with you at church, but also in your marriage, family, job, school, etc.

When we allow God into these areas of our lives we open lines of communication and avenues for God to bless and cover us. The enemy is seeking to destroy every part of our life, but when we invite God in and allow Him to have Lordship over our lives, we can rely on His power to overcome any situation.

The third key is to daily crucify your flesh and renew your mind. This is so important because our minds are so easily clogged with day-to-day activities. When we are not focused and have not surrendered our minds to the power of the Holy Spirit, we leave room for the enemy to influence our minds with negative and satanic thoughts. When we renew our minds, through prayer, reading His word, and spending time in worship; we are allowing the Holy Spirit authority over our mind. We are able to focus more on the Lord and His course for our lives.

Too Young

"I am too young" is nothing but an excuse. Let down your guard and know that the Lord does not make mistakes. If you have heard the Lord speak to you concerning your destiny and what you have been purposed to do on this earth, be open and ask Him for His provision and the wisdom to walk out your call and purpose. He has chosen you because He can trust you. It is His power that works through us to fulfill the purpose He has placed in us. You have been pre-qualified for the job, just show up and allow the Lord to train you.

Chapter Five

Lost in God's Will

No sense of direction, not knowing which way is up, which way is down? Feeling like you are going in a circle? Have you ever felt this way? I have. There have been plenty of seasons in my life when I felt lost.

One particular time, I was still active in the youth ministry in my home church and loving every moment of it. Yet I felt out of place and like there was something missing. I was considered one of the youth ministers at the church and my responsibility was to coordinate and oversee the Sunday services. During this time, we were going through a transition with some youth leaders. Many had come and gone, but we finally had a team that was stable. One of the most important concepts I stressed with the team was that the youth needed consistency.

Over the years so many people stood before them for a moment and then they were gone. The attitude among the youth was, "We are not going to get comfortable with anyone because before you know it, someone else is going to be leaving". We worked hard to ensure that our team of leaders was committed to the ministry. The ministry was very different now -- more young people were getting involved, our numbers were growing, but more importantly the young people began to grow spiritually. Although things were going good, I was still searching, because I knew that there was more that I needed to do. Staying inside the four walls was not an option for me.

About this time the Lord began revamping the vision for Faithful Followers. I kept it to myself and just wrote down what the Lord would give me. I had no clue what the Lord was doing but I continued to pray. I asked God to reveal more, but during this season the Lord was very quiet. He wasn't saying anything regarding what I was personally seeking Him for. Although He was not speaking to me in those regards, I still knew that He was close. In times like these, we have to remember what God said, *Be strong and of a good courage, fear not, nor be afraid of them: for the LORD thy God, he [it is] that doth go with thee; he will not fail thee, nor forsake thee.* [Deuteronomy 31:6]

I meditated on that scripture day and night. Crazy things began to happen. My character was being tested in ways that it had never been before and, there was an uneasy spirit that stayed with me for months. I could not explain how I felt or why I felt the way that I did. I was in a place of spiritual warfare. The enemy was trying to stop me and discourage me from doing what I love to do. I have to admit there was a point, when I was ready to walk away. I didn't have the time for foolishness and mess. But the Lord spoke to me so clearly and said, "Don't let the enemy win". That was enough for me to stay and fight. I didn't fight physically and I didn't entertain people and their negative views, I simply kept doing what the Lord called me to do. In the end, He got the glory.

Lost in God's Will

No matter who you are, when you are doing what God has called you to do, there will always be opposition and you will always have to deal with Pharisees. The Pharisees were a religious Jewish sect that was determined to uphold Hebrew law. When Jesus came on the scene, they had something negative to say about everything He did. They didn't understand who Jesus truly was and what He was on earth to do. There was a time when Jesus was going into the synagogue and He saw a man with a withered hand. Immediately the Pharisees challenged Jesus by asking if it was lawful to heal on the Sabbath day. The only reason they were asking Jesus this question, was to accuse Him. Jesus responded by saying, *What man shall there be among you, that shall have one sheep, and if it fall into a pit on the sabbath day, will he not lay hold on it, and lift [it] out?" How much then is a man better than a sheep? Wherefore it is lawful to do well on the sabbath days. When saith he to the man, Stretch forth thine hand. And he stretched [it] forth; and it was restored whole, like as the other.* [Matthew 12:11-13]

I love how Jesus handled Himself. He knew exactly what was up the sleeves of the Pharisees, yet He did not stoop to their level. He answered their question with a question to make them think, and then He did what He was supposed to do -- heal the man's hand. In spite of the opposition and the repercussions He was about to face, He stood His ground, was obedient and walked in His divine purpose. *Then the Pharisees went out, and held a council against him, how they might destroy him. But when Jesus knew [it], he withdrew himself from thence: and great multitudes followed him, and he healed them all.* [Matthew 12:14-15]

There was no stopping Jesus. He was placed on earth with a purpose for a purpose, and He fulfilled it. Just like Jesus, we are on earth with a purpose for a purpose and we must fulfill it. Remember we are not alone *and being confident of this very thing, that he which hath begun a good work in you will perform [it] until the day of Jesus Christ.* [Philippians 1:6]

Lost in God's Will

When my character was being tested and I was going through spiritual warfare, I had to stand on the promises of God, even though it was hard. You don't have to take my word for it, follow the example of Jesus, His example is the best and it will never fail you.

Just when I thought things were getting a little better, I was side tracked by what the Lord would do next. One day I was sitting in church and during the service, the Lord led me to the book of Deuteronomy. The scripture read, *Then we turned, and took our journey into the wilderness by the way of the Red sea, as the LORD spake unto me: and we compassed Mount Seir many days. And the LORD spake unto me, saying, Ye have compassed this mountain long enough: turn you northward.* [Deuteronomy 2:1-3] At that moment, I knew what the Lord was saying to me. I kept reading and reading the scripture over and over. The Lord was saying that my time was up and I needed to leave the youth ministry. This was a hard pill to swallow, because I loved the youth and the relationships I had built. How was I going to stand before them and tell them that

I was leaving? I prayed hard and asked the Lord to give me the strength. About three weeks later, the Lord had me to stand before the young people and share with them what I had been dealing with and how the Lord had instructed me to go in a different direction. It was definitely very hard, but I made it through, by the grace of God and the prayers of the leaders who I had told previously. The young people received it well, they knew that just because I was leaving the ministry, didn't mean I was not going to be a part of their lives.

And so there it was, I was no longer in the youth ministry, but still a part of my church. About a month later, the Lord gave me confirmation that it was time to leave the church. I wrote my resignation letter and sent it to all the Pastors. I first met with my uncle, Pastor Davis and a few weeks later I met with Bishop. Bishop gave me great words of wisdom. He released me and said if I ever needed to come back, I was welcomed. That is still my home church and it will always be.

Lost in God's Will

Headed in a new Direction

Now what? I began to casually visit other churches that some of my friends attended. I built relationships with the pastors and members, but I knew those weren't the churches God was sending me to. Over the years I had been invited to a church in Phenix City Alabama to preach for their youth day services. I was introduced to Pastor Noble Williams by his sister, Pastor Veta Blanding. I didn't really understand what was happening, but I began driving two hours to Phenix City. It was strange, but I felt like I had not been to church unless I was at Greater Mt. Zion. A few months earlier, I had a conversation with Pastor Williams and he encouraged me to come on board as a youth minister. This, of course, was very exciting to me, since I had just left the youth ministry at my home church and felt a little lost. One Sunday, the call was given to join the church and there I went walking down to the front. I shocked Pastor Williams, but I knew that this was the place the Lord was calling me to be. And I knew this was the pastor I was supposed to be under.

So here I am, now a member of Greater Mt. Zion. About a year later, I began working with the youth and conducting Sunday worship services. Through that process I still felt lost; however, even though I felt lost, I knew I was in the will of God. When you are in the will of God, you may not exactly know what the next step is, but rest assured He is taking you in the right direction. We just have to continue to follow Him, believing that the Lord will not lead us wrong. Do you think the Israelites knew exactly where they were and where they were headed after they had been circling Mount Seir for so many days? No, but they listened to His voice and His direction and headed North. God will not always give you the specifics of what it is He wants you to do. Sometimes He will give you piece by piece. Think about it, if God gave us the whole picture, then we would have no need of Him. God desires that we depend on Him and His direction for our life. As long as we listen to His voice, He will not lead us wrong. It is much better to be lost in God's will than lost in your own. Many of the tasks that the Lord will call you to do are not for a lifetime, but only for a season. Another important thing to know is that you must recognize when your season is over. Too many people leave an assignment prematurely or extend their stay -- both can be destructive. When you leave a task early, you forfeit your end blessing. There is a blessing in completing the task that the Lord gives you. If Jesus did not complete His task, He would have never conquered death, hell and the grave. Because He finished His assignment, we have the blessing of salvation. Finish your assignment and receive your end blessing. When you leave before your time, you are stepping out of the will of God and making your own path. When you move on to other things, you will always feel that something is left undone. In many cases, God will allow you to go your way, but will circle you back around to whatever you did not finish.

I have seen many people leave churches because of the "Two Ps,"-- politics and people. Because they left before their time and left incorrectly, God eventually brings them right back to where they started to finish what needs to be finished. Instead of having to make a full circle, stay in the race and complete it. God will give you the sufficient amount of strength to get through it. Don't quit, keep pressing and finish your assignment, so you can receive your end blessing.

Not leaving when your assignment is complete can also be damaging to your growth and those around you. This applies whether you are a minister, a boss, a teacher, any aspect of life. God plants you places to make a difference and have influence. He uses the gifts and talents He has placed in you to help benefit others, to build organizations and to help others succeed. When you have poured out all you have and God says it is time to move on, the best thing to do is to move on. If you stay beyond your time, you are as I say "running on fumes". Oftentimes you are not effective and you are holding back the new person that God is ready to release in your place.

Let me use my situation as an example. When the Lord instructed me to leave the youth ministry, I would have been spiritually damaging the youth under my leadership and holding back the person that was to come after me if I stayed. Many lives would have been affected if I had not been obedient. My own destiny would also have been delayed, because God had another group of people that I needed to share my gifts with. It is important to listen to the Spirit of God, He will never steer you wrong. Now I am serving at another church and affecting more peoples' lives. Remember that being lost in the will of God is an excellent place to be, because that means He is in control.

Chapter Six

Faithful in Another Man's Work

One of the greatest principles I live by is; "do
unto others as you would have them do unto
you". Some people call it the golden rule but this
is a lesson that Jesus taught us in the Word of
God. *And as ye would that men should do to you,
do ye also to them.* [Luke 6:31] The simplicity of this
verse is that you are to treat others how you
desire to be treated. If you desire to be loved
and respected, then you need to show love and
respect toward others. Do we always receive
from others what we give out? Not always.
However, God is watching and greater is His
reward towards us.

Faithful in Another Man's Work

The Bible teaches us that what you sow you will reap. I believe some of us miss the totality of this principle. This is not just speaking about money as so many people think, but it also speaks to how you treat others and handle another person's affairs. When you think about the goals you are trying to accomplish in life, have you ever considered giving your time, talents and treasures to another who is where you desire to be? In other words, have you sown into anyone else's life, ministry, business, family? It is important that you sow into areas you desire to reap a harvest from. For example, let's say I desire to have my own soup kitchen, a place where I can feed the hungry for free. Yes, it is good to make a business plan, and find people to partner with in the community, but it is even better that I sow into someone else who has an established soup kitchen. This is where I give of my time, talent and treasure. It would be a great benefit to me if I volunteered my services at another soup kitchen. How does this benefit me, you may ask? You benefit by gaining experience by working hands on where you want to be. You develop relationships with others in the same field of service. When God sees that you are faithful with someone else's visions and dreams, it shows Him that He can trust you with your own.

If you desire to have your own business, then work hard on the jobs that God blesses you with. If you desire to have your own ministry or church, then serve your pastor and church well. Through serving men and serving the body of Christ, we are serving God Himself. Remember what Christ said, *And the King shall answer and say unto them, Verily I say unto you, Inasmuch as ye have done [it] unto one of the least of these my brethren, ye have done [it] unto me.* [Matthew 25:40].

One of our main duties as a Christian is being a servant. If you desire to be a great leader, be a great servant. We must take our example from Jesus Christ Himself, when He taught the Disciples what being a follower of Christ was all about. He showed them by washing their feet that we must walk in humility and serve one another.

Faithful in Another Man's Work

Jesus stated, *Even as the Son of man came not to be ministered unto, but to minister and to give his life a ransom for many.* [Matthew 20:28, Mark 10:45] The word "ministered" translates to "served" as we talked about in chapter one.

I love, honor and respect my pastor. Since God has placed me under his care, it is my obligation as his spiritual daughter to do my part in helping to bring to pass the vision God has given to him. I must give of my time, I must use the gifts that God has given me and I must sow financially to my church. You must sow into the ground that you desire to receive a harvest from in own life. The Bible teaches us, *And if ye have not been faithful in that which is another man's, who shall give you that which is your own?* [Luke 16:12]

Remember to be a blessing to someone else. God blesses us to be a blessing to other people. Don't hold on to your blessings by keeping a closed fist, but release your blessings to others. By leaving your hand open you are free to receive more from God.

Chapter Seven

Dream Again

Children have such a great imagination. They are always dreaming of being something in life. I remember as a little girl in kindergarten, we used to sit in a circle and have story time, sing nursery rhymes and share what we wanted to be when we grew up. The typical answers were always a doctor, a nurse, a fireman, a policeman, a teacher. Of course, throughout life our dreams tend to change and get bigger. On the other hand, some people stop dreaming. This is one of the most distressing things to witness. When a person stops dreaming, they slowly give up on life and never reach for anything. They stay in a little comfy box and never explore the possibilities. Eleanor Roosevelt said "The future belongs to those who believe in the beauty of their dreams." Dreaming gives you a hope that is unbroken and it produces a joy in your life that is unspeakable. When you conceive wonderful things in your mind and have the faith to believe that it will come to pass, wonderful things happen in your life. God gives us dreams because He knows that the sky is the limit and that through him all things are possible. *I can do all things through Christ which strengtheneth me.* [Philippians 4:13] If you have lost faith and have become discouraged, then repeat this scripture until you believe again.

Some of the things that cause us to stop dreaming are people speaking negative things into our lives. One of the most frequent dream killers of children is parents who tell their kids they will never be anything. This plants a seed in a child's life that can affect him forever. However, we have the power of God to reverse the curse. Parents that have stopped dreaming and settled for mediocrity tend to be bitter and do not want to see others succeed. They feel if they can't do it then neither can their children. But this is a lie from the pit of hell. *Nay, in all these things we are more than conquerors through him that loved us.* [Romans 8:37] You have to keep pushing and pressing through all the negativity around you and not allow anyone to kill your dreams.

Another thing that keeps people from dreaming is past failures. When people fail at a task it can do one of two things: it will push them to keep trying until it comes to pass, or it can cause discouragement. Once discouragement takes root, a person will more than likely give up. We have to remember even in our failures we are victorious. *But thanks [be] to God, which giveth us the victory through our Lord Jesus Christ. Therefore, my beloved brethren, be ye stedfast, unmoveable, always abounding in the work of the Lord, forasmuch as ye know that your labour is not in vain in the Lord.* [1Corinthians 15:57-58]

Our failures teach us valuable lessons. Failure builds our character and perseverance. It helps us to depend on the power of God and to humble ourselves before Him. Failure also teaches us that we can continue to exist. Failure is not the end of the world, but a force to push us to get up and succeed.

Dream Again

These scriptures are not just for you to read, but to serve as encouragement to you. Meditate on these scriptures until you begin to feel your dreams resurrect and you believe that without a shadow of a doubt that you can accomplish it. Dr. Dale E. Turner states,"Dreams are renewable. No matter what our age or condition, there are still untapped possibilities within us and new beauty waiting to be born."

Do not let age cripple you. If you had a dream at the age of twelve and you are now sixty, go for it! It is never too late. Remember, with Christ you can do all things!

Chapter eight is all for you. Write a chapter about your dream. Who knows it will probably turn into book. Be encouraged my brother and my sister. You have been called by God to do great and wonderful things for the kingdom. Allow Him to lead you on this journey. With Him you can't go wrong.

This is where my pen stops writing and you complete the book.

Chapter Eight

My Dream

My dream is:

Prayer For You

Heavenly Father, I thank you for those who have taken time to read this book. I pray a special blessing upon their life. It is my prayer that if my brother or sister does not know their purpose in life speak to them as you did to me. Open their ears and hearts to hear and receive from You. Open their eyes that they can see the things You are trying to show them.

My prayer is as they step out on faith, and walk in obedience unto You, Lord that You will bless everything they set out to do for You. I decree and declare your sons and daughters will walk in their callings, and bring glory to Your name in everything that they do. Lord, please bless them in a special way today as they step out on faith.
In Jesus name I pray.
Amen

JSB Ministries

How to contact us:

By Mail:

P.O. Box 465001
Lawrenceville, Georgia 30042
USA

By Phone:

Voice: 404.910.3957

By Internet:

Email: jsbministriesinc@gmail.com
Websites: www.wix.com/jborges11/jsbministries
                  www.faithfulfollowersministries.com

Made in the USA
Charleston, SC
07 October 2013